LYME LANDSCAPE WITH FIGURES

LYME LANDSCAPE WITH FIGURES

Muriel A. Arber

DORSET BOOKS

All proceeds from this book have most kindly been donated to the Friends of Lyme Regis Museum.

First published in Great Britain in 1988 by Dorset Books

Copyright © Muriel A. Arber, 1988
Illustrations © Muriel A. Arber (except p. 62)

The photograph on p.62 is reproduced by permission of Brenda Lang.

ISBN: 1 871164 00 1

All rights reserved. No part of this publication may be reproduced, stored in a retrieval system, or transmitted in any form or by any means, electronic, mechanical, photocopying, recording or otherwise, without the prior permission of the copyright holder.

British Library Cataloguing-in-Publication Data
Arber, Muriel A.
   Lyme landscape with figures
   1. Dorset. Lyme Regis, 1920–1950. Biographies.
   I. Title
   942.3'31

Printed and bound in Great Britain by A. Wheaton & Co. Ltd

DORSET BOOKS

An imprint of Wheaton Publishers Ltd, a member of Maxwell Pergamon Publishing Corporation plc

Wheaton Publishers Ltd
Hennock Road, Marsh Barton, Exeter, Devon EX2 8RP
Tel: 0392 74121; Telex 42794 (WHEATN G)

SALES

Direct sales enquiries to Dorset Books at the address above.
Trade sales to: Town & Country Books, P.O. Box 31, Newton Abbot, Devon TQ12 5AQ. Tel: 08047 2690

Cover illustration: **The Cobb in 1927**

For
John Fowles
who encouraged me to write these
'Memoiries'

FOREWORD

A visitor to Lyme many years ago — like Jane Austen, from Bath — evoked a goddess of place, 'a genius of this shore', and drily attributed the inspiration for the long satiric poem that resulted, *The Lymiad*, to this local deity, who was complaining that no one seemed able to save Lyme 'from the sad wreck of dark Oblivion's wave'. I must not suggest that Muriel Arber was ever guilty, like the supposed goddess, of walking round Cobb Bay wearing a zone of limpet shells, a wig of seaweed and a pyritized ammonite perched on her head as a diadem; but I hope she will not mind being compared to Lymia, that tutelary spirit of place. She is certainly likened by her long knowledge of Lyme and always transparent affection for it, characteristically transmitted with the enthusiasm of someone a quarter of her real age. But with the fun-poking poetess, though Muriel writes poetry herself, the comparison stops. Nothing is further from her than the satire, the mocking of the small and provincial, that is the basic attitude of *The Lymiad*. This is emphatically a tribute of love, not a Regency exhibition of finer taste or greater knowledge of the world than Lyme could ever boast.

As curator of the Lyme Regis Museum, I may say that Muriel has become over the years the great living authority on our twentieth-century past, the person to whom one refers all recent historical problems and to whom one gratefully submits in draft all written nowadays on Lyme. In that freely given help she perhaps most resembles one of her grandfathers. I remember asking, the first time we met, if she was by any chance descended from Edward Arber; to hear that she is in fact his grand-daughter. You may not have heard of him, but all book-collectors will know of the long and invaluable series of meticulously edited ancient texts he produced in Victorian times. Muriel's corrections are always kind but, aided by a remarkable memory, nevertheless strict and just as meticulous as were her grandfather's. Her *imprimatur*, it may be printed, is a precious asset, an amateur curator's dream. On local geology, especially landslipping, she is of course unsurpassed; and north Devon has benefited as much as Lyme from the tradition of scrupulous scholarship that she and both her parents so well embody.

I think I only once truly upset her. That was in a little record I had made of local landslip disasters. The upsetting was not so much because of the various scientific and historical errors, but to do with the less than kind terms I used in connection with past blunders of local government and land-owners. One great privilege of knowing Muriel is encountering her gentleness, her good manners in an age so without them, and not least her sense of humour.

A story she does not include here concerns a remark once made to her in Charmouth by Mrs Lang, wife of the distinguished geologist: 'You like Lyme, don't you, Muriel?' As Muriel's voice makes very plain in recounting it, it was not as innocent as it may seem; but only too clearly implied, true to an aged rivalry between two ancient neighbours, a lamentable defect of taste in an otherwise acceptable person. Here, at any rate, is why Muriel perversely likes Lyme; and, as will be clear, why Lyme likes her. This book has been several years in writing. Its modesty, its affectionate recalls and fascinating memories, doubly valuable in this time when 'dark Oblivion's wave' seems more than ever flooding over us, are proof that those years have been well spent.

We have always in the past referred to it as her 'Memoiries', a blend of memoirs and memories. Muriel has in the end preferred the present title, but I think that original half-playful working name gives a good clue to the nostalgic charm of this image of a Lyme and its inhabitants, both humble and more celebrated, both 'foreign' and Lyme-born, now already largely gone.

John Fowles, 1988

CHAPTER 1

I fell in love with Lyme once and for all just before four o'clock in the afternoon of Wednesday, 10 April 1922. Four years later, in a school essay for which I had chosen Lyme as the subject, I said 'to describe the whole of Lyme fully would be the task of a lifetime'. A lifetime has passed since then, and what I have written here is only my memories of the town and its surroundings, and of those whom I knew there in earlier days.

That holiday in 1922, when, at the age of eight, I was brought to Lyme by my mother, was the first occasion that any of our family had ever stayed for more than a few days in the town itself. As a girl, my mother had spent some weeks in Uplyme, and her mother, in her youth, had stayed in Charmouth. I have my grandmother's diary of this Charmouth holiday in 1874, when a large party of family and friends spent four weeks in the village. They bathed and they went for long walks, on various occasions going through what they called 'Fairy Glen'. The boys played cricket and one of them walked to Lyme to see the regatta. They all went to watch the cricket match between Charmouth 'town' and visitors, which the visitors won; on another occasion the Charmouth visitors were victorious over Whitchurch by sixty runs, but Whitchurch later won a match against Charmouth.

One day they went by wagonette to Beer and on another occasion they had an outing by 'omnibus' and wagonette to the Landslip. They seem to have had some acquaintance with the Colfox family at Bridport, whom they visited at Westmead, and they went to a croquet party and dance at their house 'at Rax'. They also shared a picnic with them at Lambert's Castle. My great-grandfather, Benjamin Brecknell Turner, was an amateur photographer, having a licence from Fox-Talbot; some of his work is now in the collection of the Victoria and Albert Museum. While they were staying at Charmouth he took photographs of Chideock, but unfortunately I have never seen them.

At the end of the holiday, the family returned to what was by then their home on Tulse Hill in London. Among their friends were Miss Gould and her sister, who were related to John Gould, but I never heard mention of his connection with Lyme. B.B. Turner, who was at one time Master of the Tallow-Chandlers' Company, still had his factory and shop in the Haymarket, where he made soap and candles. All his children had been born in the Haymarket, within sound of Bow bells, so they were true Cockneys.

My grandmother, Agnes Lucy, was his younger daughter; she married H.R. Robertson, an artist specializing in landscape; their eldest daughter, Agnes, was my mother. The Robertson family had very little money but they always had long summer holidays, as my grandfather spent the time in the country sketching landscapes in water-colour, to serve as the basis for the oil-paintings which he worked on during the rest of the year at Steele's Studios on Haverstock Hill in London. The family usually stayed either in the country or at a little distance inland from the sea, partly for economy but also because my grandfather considered that the sea halved the area available for walks. In 1899 they spent four weeks at Uplyme, in lodgings at the house called the Warren, which has since been renamed Mulberry, at the foot of Rhode Lane. The back part of the house was then thatched, but it has now been tiled. I have a photograph of one of my aunts, Janet Robertson, sitting on the beach at Lyme; I believe that it was taken under Church Cliffs. The sharpness of the limestone beds is in marked contrast to conditions today. The only paintings done by my grandfather on this holiday that I have ever seen were one of the Cobb and a view of the Dorset coast from Church Cliffs.

A family of London friends, Mrs Weekley and her daughters, were staying in Lyme at the same time, I believe in one of the cottages that have now been demolished at the end of Coombe Street next to Gosling Bridge. My mother said that Coombe Street in those days was very stuffy in high summer, and even in their lodgings at Uplyme my grandmother suffered from a quinsy. In consequence, when my mother later brought me to Lyme, we always came in the spring.

There was a strong family tradition of collecting and pressing flowers, and by the time of this early holiday at Uplyme my mother was already passionately interested in botany. Miss Gulielma ('Gulie') Lister, of Lyme, had visited North London Collegiate School, where my mother was a pupil, and, discovering her enthusiasm, gave her a little collection of exquisitely mounted Mycetozoa (the Myxomycetes or slime-moulds) on which she was working with her father, Arthur Lister. This was the beginning of a friendship with the Lister family which has extended through the generations to the present day.

Janet Robertson, Lyme Regis, 1899

My mother took her degree in botany, geology and other scientific subjects at University College, London and then at Newnham College, Cambridge. While she was at Newnham one of her closest friends was Dorothea ('Dolly') Marryat, who was of the same family as Captain Marryat, author of *Mr Midshipman Easy* and *The Children of the New Forest*. Dolly Marryat became engaged to Joseph Jackson Lister, a zoologist and a Fellow of the Royal Society; he was a brother of Gulielma, and thus my mother established a second link of friendship with the Lister family.

After leaving Newnham, my mother went to Ethel Sargant's private botanical laboratory at Reigate for a year and then returned to University College to do research in botany and to teach, until her marriage to Edward Alexander Newell Arber in 1909, which brought her back to Cambridge where she lived until her death in 1960. Her botanical work, which after her marriage she published under the name of Agnes Arber, was in two main fields: the history of botany, on which her writing included a book on *Herbals*, and plant morphology, on which she wrote many papers, and several books published by Cambridge University Press. In 1946 she was the third woman ever to be elected F.R.S., and she was awarded the Linnean Gold Medal in 1947. In the latter part of her life, her interests became more and more philosophical, and it was on philosophy that she published her last books, *The Mind and the Eye* and *The Manifold and the One*. She has an entry in the *Dictionary of National Biography*.

My father, Newell Arber, was the elder son of Professor Edward Arber who published pioneer reprints of English texts from Caxton to Addison, as well as of bibliographical records. Edward Arber too is included in the *Dictionary of National Biography*. He had a slight literary link with Devon, for it was on his reprint of the accounts by Sir Walter Raleigh and others of the last fight of the *Revenge* that Tennyson based his 'Ballad'.

Newell Arber was a palaeobotanist and geologist, and was Demonstrator in Palaeobotany at the Sedgwick Museum, Cambridge. He too published many scientific papers and books, on palaeobotany, on Alpine flowers and on coastal geology and scenery. In the course of establishing the age of the Culm Measures of north Devon by means of their fossil flora, he became fascinated by the coastal waterfalls, and this led to his study of the cliffs in his book *The Coast Scenery of North Devon*. When this had been written, he considered making a corresponding study of south Devon, but he found that at that date, just before the First World War, it was impracticable because so much of the rugged coast of south-west Devon was in private hands and thus difficult of access. He and my mother stayed briefly at the Cups Hotel in

Lyme in 1912, but the softness of the rocks here was such a marked contrast to the wild northern coast of Devon that he was not attracted by it.

He died at the age of forty-eight in 1918, just before my fifth birthday. My parents had been very poor and much of my father's advisory work on coalfield prospecting, especially in Kent, had come to an end with the outbreak of war in 1914. The years that followed his death were financially difficult and our holidays were spent in the Fens near Cambridge or on the Norfolk coast; however, I was once taken to Harrogate when my mother was ordered to go there for a rheumatism cure. Apart from Torquay and Saunton, to both of which I had been taken when I was two years old, too young to appreciate them fully, Harrogate was by far the most romantic place I had seen in my life, and when I was taught the Lord's Prayer shortly afterwards, I firmly believed it to say 'Harrogate be thy name', which seemed to me to be most appropriate.

We stayed on another occasion with a friend of my mother's who had an old farmhouse in the Sussex Weald, where I was enthralled by the distant scarp of the South Downs. My longing to go to the Downs and climb them was not known till afterwards, when it was generously fulfilled on a later occasion. On this first visit I found, framed on a wall, the last verse of Kipling's 'Sussex', beginning:

> God gives all men all earth to love,
> But since man's heart is small
> Ordains for each one spot shall prove
> Beloved over all.

It was years before I discovered the poem as a whole, but this verse went straight to the depths of my nature. I announced that I wanted to write to Kipling to tell him what it meant to me and I was allowed to do so; I believe that my mother put in a covering note to say that my letter was entirely unprompted. I had a charming reply from him, speaking of the pleasure of life in Sussex and telling me of his farm and its calves and the goslings in his orchard.

I was thus ready for further impressions of places, but circumstances gave no scope for distant holidays. Then, when I was eight, Dolly Lister received a legacy and decided that she would make it possible for my mother to take me for a holiday at Lyme, where Gulie Lister and her sisters always spent the spring and summer at Highcliff. She sent my mother a cheque for twenty-five pounds; my mother, feeling that she could not be thus beholden, burnt it. I did not fully understand what was going on, but I watched my mother putting it into the fire and I was much impressed. By return of post there came another cheque from Dolly Lister with the simple message 'Why do you waste my cheques?' My mother capitulated and we went by train to Lyme on 10 April 1922. Gulie Lister's sister Bella had found us lodgings with Mrs Case at Guildhall House, and at the station we left our luggage to follow in a cart while we walked down to Bridge Street. We were on the left-hand pavement, just above Hill Road, when we came to the sudden vista of Silver Street, then lined with picturesque cottages many of which have since been swept away, while below were the roofs of the town with the sea beyond. I let out a loud shout of rapture, but this was 1922 and I can still hear my mother saying, 'Darling, you really mustn't make so much noise'. I suppressed my ecstasy, but I have been shouting about Lyme ever since. My mother did not know that at that moment I had found the key to the whole future of my life; in later years she always laughed at her unwitting attempt to stem the tide.

CHAPTER 2

Guildhall House in Bridge Street is in the heart of old Lyme, almost on Gun Cliff, within sound of the sea, and in a storm during that first fortnight I remember the spray coming right over the topmost pinnacles of the Guildhall and Museum. Our bedroom window looked down into Cockmoil Square and on to the door of the old lock-up. Our sitting-room was on the ground floor and fitted triangularly into the corner between Bridge Street and the first house in Church Street. Opposite was the open lower floor of the Guildhall; my impression is that the stocks and the old fire-engine still stood here in 1922, but they were certainly in the Museum by 1923.

The house was the home of Mr and Mrs Charlie Case; she was from Chideock and he was of the builders' family in Lyme. He had brought goods by cart from Axminster before the railway came. Their son Bert, who was a carpenter, had married Ada, the daughter of Samuel Govier, Whistler's 'Master Smith of Lyme Regis'; they were the parents of Mr Eddie Case of Broad Street and I am grateful to him for information about the family. Mr and Mrs Case's daughter Edie was Mrs Watson, mother of Mr Jack Watson of Watson's Garage, which replaced Govier's smithy; she was widowed early and she later became Mrs Burton. Another daughter, Bessie, who was Mrs Elliott, died young; I used to play with her little girl, Joan, who was about my age and who later became Mrs Pope. An unmarried daughter, Nellie, who lived at home, took part in the annual performances of the Operatic Society, but she died a few years after we first knew the family.

My mother succeeded in eking out Dolly Lister's gift so that we had not only that first fortnight in 1922 but three weeks in 1923 and, I think, part of our 1924 holiday as her guests. Even after that we came every spring. From 1923 onwards we regularly stayed for three weeks, but in 1925 I had been unwell during the winter and we had a blissful fourth week; the Easter

Bridge Street, 1927: *Guildhall House (only partly visible) is the last (white) house on the left*

Mr and Mrs Case, 1927

holidays at the Perse School in Cambridge were long enough to make this possible. That year we were joined for a week by my aunt Janet Robertson, who had a room in Mrs Pocock's Bell Cliff Boarding House, the room itself being over Isbell's shop, which is now the Toby Jug. After our fifth stay at Guildhall House, Mr and Mrs Case moved to 50 Church Street, which was then called Freeman House but has now been renamed Marlray, and we stayed there with them in 1927 and 1928. In later years we always went there to see Mrs Case; I recorded in my diary that she had the sweetest voice I had ever heard. We were in Lyme when she died in 1938, at a time when they still tolled the passing-bell.

Between 1928 and 1932, I was first at boarding-school and then having coaching at home for the Newnham entrance examination, and we spent our spring holidays on the Isle of Wight, on Dartmoor and at Bideford in north Devon, only returning to Lyme in May 1932 when we stayed for a fortnight in lodgings with Mrs Goldsworthy at 10 Marine Parade. In July 1933, when I was recovering from a tonsil operation, we had four weeks in June and early July with Mrs Cook at Cedar Cottage on East Cliff. There was a garden extending to the edge of the cliff and at the end a raised seat overlooked the sea. Here I taught myself to play a celluloid flageolet and when I had mastered 'Three blind mice' the cat came and rubbed itself against me. I spent many hours on the lawn and on the seat, but within the next twenty years the seaward half of the garden had slipped down the cliff.

In 1934 we went for the first time to Mrs Grattan at the Royal Standard by the Cobb. Here we returned every spring until the war, after which my mother ceased to go away for holidays, and ever since 1940 I have stayed alone in hotels, first at the Stile House, then at the Buena Vista, and since 1951 at the Alexandra.

When I was nine years old, in the winter between our first and second visits to Lyme, I read for the first time Angela Brazil's *A Fortunate Term*. I enjoyed all her books, but this one was far more than a mere school story. In essence it is a book about Devon, to which two sisters are sent for the sake of the health of the elder. Chagmouth, the Devon village with which they fall in love, is in fact modelled on Polperro over the Cornish border and the scenery is that of a rocky coast; nevertheless the spirit of the place, before it had been discovered by tourists, and the sense of spring and enhanced life were what I had experienced at Lyme. Every first day of February I still relive the day of their first visit to Chagmouth, and this book is one which will go with me when I have to reduce my possessions to the confines of one room in an old people's home.

When I was a child, the day of the journey to Lyme was second only to Christmas Day itself; I

Church Street, 1927: *Freeman House (as it was then called) is the last (white) house on the right*

think I enjoyed it even more than my birthday. I sewed new clothes for those of my dolls who were chosen for the special privilege of a holiday at Lyme. I had invested one doll, Amy, with a 'naughty' character and she did not come; then one year she 'reformed' and was rewarded by Lyme.

In a changing world one of the few unchanging things has been the eleven o'clock train from Waterloo; the time has varied by a few minutes, but even now it leaves at ten minutes past eleven. We always took it. In 1924 a Cambridge friend of my mother's, Mrs Willis, brought her daughter Anita, who was about my age, for a holiday at Lyme at the same time as ours; they stayed at Argyle House. They travelled on the one o'clock from Waterloo and I remember my amazement that anyone could voluntarily forego arriving in time for the first walk on the Cobb after tea.

We always took the train from Cambridge to King's Cross and thence went by taxi to Waterloo. As we crossed London there were many landmarks which became hallowed with a touch of Lyme: the Quantock Laundry, with its West Country name, in a Bloomsbury street; the shot tower; the basket-work kangaroo that hung outside a shop south of Waterloo Bridge; and above all the red lion of the Lambeth brewery.

At Waterloo there was a Newfoundland or St Bernard dog with a collecting box strapped to his back, who used to be brought round for contributions to the railway orphanage and I was always given a penny to put into his box. Some of the railway engines one saw were of the King Arthur class, with their romantic names, appropriate for such a journey. As the train left London and crossed Surrey it passed through one or two deep cuttings with fir trees and in one of these I always asked the traditional question, 'Where shall we go for the first walk tomorrow?', knowing that I should receive the looked-for reply, 'The Charmouth footpath'.

The journey was punctuated by landmarks. The motor-racing track was still in existence at Brooklands. At Old Basing one could see the ruins of the house where Thomas Johnson, the translator of Gerard's *Herbal*, was killed during a siege of the house in the Civil War. We also passed the Sorbo factory whence had come my ball which bounced so much more satisfactorily than the harder balls of my earlier childhood. In the fields were the brewery advertisements with the words 'You are now approaching the Strong country', 'You are now in the Strong country', and so on. Junipers were to be seen on Salisbury Plain and then came Salisbury Cathedral spire, marking what I called to myself 'the gateway to the west'. I was utterly unaware of the railway-poster banality of this phrase, which was all my own, and to my intense delight when I later became a student of geology at Cambridge I discovered that the position of Salisbury at the head of the Vale of Wardour does make it geologically the true 'gateway to the west', where the Jurassic rocks of Somerset and Dorset first outcrop below the chalk.

We had to change at Salisbury and we always ate a picnic lunch soon afterwards, as we passed the thatched stone-built villages that were the real beginning of the holiday. Wilton, Dinton, Tisbury, Semley, Gillingham, Templecombe, Milborne Port, Sherborne, Yeovil Junction, Sutton Bingham, Crewkerne, Chard and Axminster; the names are a roll-call leading to the final glory of the change for Lyme. Once there was a small boy in the same compartment who was most excited when we passed the 'home of Petter oil engines' at Yeovil. At Sherborne there was the Abbey; Chard Junction was heralded by a glimpse of Forde Abbey; the meandering Axe led to Axminster and the crossing of the line by the foot-bridge to the little railway to paradise. Round the hills it ran, past fields in which there were always lambs, through woods still bare of leaves but primrose-carpeted, and then to the station with the name-board 'Combpyne for the Landslip', then by the cutting to the Shapwick valley, where for years in the 1930s and 1940s there was always a turkey-cock spreading his tail in one of the yards of Shapwick Grange. And then came the most thrilling moment of all: the crossing of Cannington Viaduct. There were views up and down the valleys, with king-cups in Alder Grove; then the train wound along the hillside and past some houses with a glimpse down into Uplyme. Back into Dorset and under the bridge, and the moment arrived when the great range of cliffs came into sight at last, past Golden Cap to Portland Bill.

My mother loved these holidays but she did not share the depth of my passion for Lyme and when my aunt Janet suggested one year that we should instead join her for a holiday in the Lake District, my mother was quite prepared to fall in with the plan. I was heart-broken, and I remember my private thought, constantly repeated to myself, 'I can't be unfaithful to Lyme'. Although I expressed it thus, I had no sense of obligation, but merely a feeling that I could not tear myself away. At last my mother realized the depth of my distress and the Lake District plan was abandoned, though I fancy that my aunt thought it a great pity that I clung so to Lyme.

The end of each holiday was as grievous as the beginning was joyful. Sitting in the train, awaiting the moment of departure and the last glimpse of the cliffs, I once read a fanciful railway-poster that began 'There was a merchant of Purbeck…'. This was my first introduction to the idea of Purbeck, which I realized was somewhere in Dorset, and it sowed the seed of a desire to go there too. I was always in a state of mourning on my return home, feeling that nothing else mattered but Lyme; I remember looking at the dressing-gown hanging on my bedroom door and thinking 'That dressing-gown was in Lyme this morning', investing it with a certain sacred quality. I must have been an intolerable companion for my mother until the acute Lyme-sickness had subsided. I recognised some of the absurdity of my state of mind, for I fully appreciated the comedy one year when, during our first tea after arrival at Lyme, I exclaimed rapturously, 'How lovely the Lyme bread is!', to which my mother replied, 'It's the bread I brought from home, dear.'

CHAPTER 3

In the early 1920s Lyme was of course a much smaller town than it is now and there was none of the present infilling on the outskirts. Up the Charmouth Road, there were no buildings above the Tudbold Almshouses, apart from Summerhill, Cumberland Cottage, the cemetery, Fairfield and the cottages opposite, and finally the old toll-house known as Frost's Cottage, since demolished, the name surviving in Frost's Corner. Charmouth Road echoed with the raucous cry of peacocks kept in what was then a yard opposite the London Inn. The council estate between Charmouth Road, Colway Lane and the river had not yet been built. There was only one house on the north side of Pound Street, above Langmoor Cottage, and there was none of the modern building off Haye Lane and Clappentail Lane. Coram Avenue did not exist and there were no houses in Pine Walk; the only houses in the Sidmouth Road area were those near the main road. Through the archway that opened into the garden of Little Cliff (now renamed Upper Cobb), which was the home of the architect Arnold Mitchell, one could glimpse an old lead cistern, and a figure which to me has always been 'That one little leaden lad' of de la Mare's 'The Sunken Garden'.

The old Assembly Rooms had been converted into a cinema, standing on what is now the Cobb Gate car park at the foot of Bell Cliff. On the site of the present Post Office in Broad Street there stood until 1928 an old house which was where George Roberts had his school, and below it, where Woolworth's now stands, was the forge belonging to Whistler's Master Smith. Visitors were allowed to enter and in 1922 I was taken to see the forge at work.

In 1933 the land by the Woodmead Halls, now the site of the Leisure Centre, was being levelled for tennis courts and we heard that the workmen were finding shot from the siege of Lyme. We went up there and were shown a piece of shot which we bought from the men, but that evening we went back alone and I found two pieces which had never been touched by hand since they were fired in the siege.

CHAPTER 3

Broad Street, looking down, 1927

Coombe Street, 1928, *showing Mr Grattan's butcher's shop*

Sherborne Lane, 1927

CHAPTER 3

Marine Parade, 1927: *the chimneys of the old cement works are to be seen behind the Cobb*

Madeira Cottage, 1928, *before the building of Little Madeira*

The Cobb Gate, 1927, *with the old Assembly Rooms (converted into a cinema)*

CHAPTER 3

Broad Street, looking up, 1927

On 15 April 1922, during the first week I ever spent at Lyme, there was a fierce gale, and the lifeboat was launched. This was the *Thomas Masterman Hardy*, the last large lifeboat with a crew of thirteen to be stationed at Lyme. She stood by the disabled sailing vessel *Jessie Norcross*, off the Chesil Beach. I was already in bed and I thought that the sound of the maroons was a motor cycle back-firing, but my mother had gone for an evening walk to the Cobb and saw the launch which she described in her diary:

> Just as I got to the lifeboat house a man came out and sent off two rockets. Then the men assembled, got into their oilskins and the life jackets they put on over their heads. Mostly looking rather inexpressive – one jolly-looking man laughing and joking – one old pale bearded man looking *cold* and miserable. It was most thrilling to see the carriage with the boat on it drawn out by two ropes pulled by men and turned down the shingle bank to the harbour. The men then got in and the carriage was run down into the sea – men going deep with it, and then run off the carriage. It was rowed across the harbour and then the sails were put up. It went up and down in the most sickening way in the open sea.

The *Jessie Norcross* was eventually taken in tow by two tugs from Weymouth and the Lyme lifeboat returned after twelve hours at sea.

CHAPTER 4

The most obvious walk, statutory on the first morning of every holiday, was by the 'Charmouth footpath', leading from the corner of Charmouth Road and Spittles Lane diagonally across the fields to join the old coach road above. Slipping of the Black Ven cliff has now destroyed almost all of this footpath, and an upper outlet has been made further west into the old coach road under Rhodehorn Plantation; the National Trust has designated this area the Spittles, although the name properly belongs to the cliff below. The ground has subsided into miniature scarps and chasms, while the stream that drains the undercliff above now flows as a watercourse down what was once the path where it joins the old coach road. Eastward of this point, the coach road has vanished into space, but it used to lead on through the Devil's Bellows and down into Charmouth by the Old Lyme Road, the top of which is now barricaded off. Buses went that way until 1924, although later a boatman who took us for a row said that from the sea the road was seen to be dangerously undercut. After the road had become impassable to traffic, one could still scramble up the broken part on foot, and until 1938 it remained possible to walk along to Charmouth, skirting the edge of the great amphitheatre west of the Devil's Bellows; but by 1939 the road had been completely eaten away at this point. After that, one could still use the old Roman road over the cliff-top till that too was cut by slipping in 1958.

So long as one could still follow the Charmouth footpath across the fields, one thing which remained unaltered was the great size of the daisies which grew there. It was below the stile in the third field up that my mother found the 'hen-and-chicken' daisies, in which there is an extra ring of secondary daisies produced within the main flower-head. Her drawing of this specimen was later reproduced in Fig. 30 of her book *The Natural Philosophy of Plant Form*.

On the other side of the town, the walk through Holmbush Fields to Ware Cliffs was entirely rural; the Holmbush car park was a green field of irregular surface, used for grazing. On the seaward side of Pine Walk there was a meadow in which Shetland ponies were kept, to the delight of a child, while the absence of buildings allowed a beautiful view of the coast. The trees will always be to me those of which Flecker wrote in 'Brumana':

> .... preserve me the last lines
> Of that long saga which you sung me, pines,
> When, lonely boy, beneath the chosen tree
> I listened, with my eyes upon the sea.

Immediately beyond Pine Walk the steep step is a result of recent slipping, but otherwise the path across the fields has changed comparatively little. The stream which drained the Ware reservoir formed what, as a child, I christened Pixie Pool, under overhanging trees; there was always a strongly reddish tinge to the water there but I have never known the cause of this. The seat on the Knap was there, and we called it Seagull Seat; on the first evening this was always the final point of the walk which began along the Cobb.

As a child at home in Cambridge, in the hour before sleep came, I used to tell myself a long story about an imaginary family who lived in an ideal house which I invented in the further Holmbush Fields; they had a boat in which they performed an amateur lifeboat rescue. When I grew older, the last field before the county boundary became for me the setting of Swinburne's 'Forsaken Garden', 'in a coign of the cliff between lowland and highland'. Although the sea is not encroaching on the land, the land is falling into the sea, making partly applicable the last verse of the poem:

> Till the slow sea rise and the sheer cliff crumble,
>   Till terrace and meadow the deep gulfs drink,
> Till the strength of the waves of the high tides humble
>   The fields that lessen, the rocks that shrink.

As the footpath leads into Devon, the county boundary used to be marked by double gates; the path was often flooded at this point. Beyond Ware Lane, in old days, rabbits kept the undercliff comparatively clear, before their numbers had been reduced by myxomatosis. Donkey Green was then an open space with a grassy mound near it known as the Giant's

Grave. Ames's Wall at Pinhay was still standing on either side of the path; half-way along it one could emerge on to the grassy slopes of Pinhay Warren overlooking the sea. Beyond the Wall, the main path led on for a stretch which was always carpeted with pine-needles and deliciously springy underfoot; then there was a little plateau, hidden by bushes, seaward of the path, from which one got a marvellously peaceful view back to the eastern side of Pinhay Bay, and which seemed remote from everything in the world except bird-song and the sound of the sea. One could easily climb down to the Bay by the steps which have now been buried under a mud-flow. At Pinhay the path descended to a valley that echoed to the beat of the ram which pumped water to Pinhay House, and soon one was within sound of the chimes of the clock on the castellated mansion of Rousdon, which had not yet become Allhallows School.

We distinguished between the Undercliff, within easy reach of Lyme, and the Landslip, which is in fact the undercliff on the seaward side of Goat Island. We were not then aware of the existence of Goat Island and the Chasm. When I was still too young to walk the whole length of the path, we used to picnic each year at the Landslip, taking the train to Combpyne station and walking thence by lanes to Dowlands Farm. The lanes were deep, with no view, and to a child the walk seemed endless, so my mother used to invent stories to keep me going. At the farm we bought our sixpenny tickets and then followed the track down to the undercliff. We ate our lunch there and then wandered about for the afternoon, before having tea at Mrs Gapper's cottage. Rough wooden benches and tables stood under the trees, and Mrs Gapper's daughter, Annie, came to take the orders and returned with trays laden with tea, bread and butter, jam and cake, all of which she must have fetched from Seaton or Axmouth several miles away along the paths. I have never seen so many chaffinches as there were in that cottage garden; they hopped on the tables, sure of receiving crumbs, and flew about everywhere, undeterred by the presence of Mrs Gapper's white cat. After tea we made our way down the rough path to the shore, a place of sublime peace. Here I scrambled among the great boulders of fallen Greensand and the slabs of Lias. Afterwards we walked back to Combpyne station and took the train back to Lyme.

In later years, we always used to spend one day of the holiday walking right through the Landslip from Ware Cliffs to Axmouth. We usually ate our lunch beside a stream which for some reason emerged pulsating beside the path; it was beyond the valley containing the Pinhay ram, but it must have had some mechanical, or perhaps accidental, control. Again we had tea at the cottage before the walk back; occasionally we took the bus back from Seaton. Sometimes we approached the Landslip along the Sidmouth road, turning down at Charton Cross and

Mrs Gapper's cottage,
Dowlands Landslip, 1928

CHAPTER 4

Muriel Arber on the shore below Mrs Gapper's cottage, 1927

Agnes Arber by the landslip path, 1928

following Charton Goyle, but we believed that we were trespassing and gave up using this route. When I had begun to study the geology of the slipping, we sometimes went through Dowlands Farm and along the cliff-top to get the breath-taking view of the Chasm and Goat Island. It was not until after the area had become a National Nature Reserve that, on 21 April 1958, a red-letter day in my life, I was actually taken up on to Goat Island by Laurie Pritchard, the Warden, and Tom Wallace of Allhallows School.

In early days, the third 'basic' walk at Lyme was up the valley. We always followed Lynch Walk, past what we called the Lepers' Well, to Gosling Bridge. Beyond Mill Green there was still a cottage at Hatchett between the path and the river, on a site which is now an open green. Beyond Horn Bridge were the fields and on one of them tennis courts had been constructed at Middle Mill. The last field before the old Uplyme Mill has always had a springiness underfoot where the path crosses the alluvium. From the mill we used to follow Mill Lane, which Gulie Lister taught us to call the Packhorse Road, that ancient hollow track leading to Waterside.

Gulie Lister also showed us the footpath that led from Shire Lane, near Upper Knapps, down into Uplyme, through the fields that she called Paradise. She told us, too, of the legend of Haye Lane: how a great black dog used to appear and run along till he came to the Black Dog Inn, where he would run up into the attics and vanish. I understood that he had never been seen since the inn was rebuilt. I have since heard that there are other black dog legends in Devon, and that sometimes smugglers may have used the stories and set dogs to run along the lanes so as to discourage people from frequenting their haunts.

In 1924, when Mrs Willis and Anita were also staying in Lyme, Anita had riding lessons from Mr Warren in Coombe Street. I had always longed to learn to ride but it was too expensive; however, in the following year, after a winter in which I had been ill, my mother arranged for me to have lessons with Miss Gladys Stapleforth of the Black Dog Inn. I went for a ride almost every day; sometimes I was taken by myself, sometimes with other children, amongst whom I remember Dr Lumsden's daughter, Jean. On one occasion there was a boy from St Albans, which was then a preparatory school, and another time a boy from A.S. Neill's school which was then in the Charmouth Road at Summerhill, a name which the school retained after it left Lyme.

Through these rides, and Miss Stapleforth's knowledge of all the bridle-paths, I came to know far more of the country: Dragon's Hill and Hole Common, St Mary's, Woolly and Trinity Hill, Cathole and Woodhouse Hill, Holcombe, Cannington and Rocombe, and I then introduced

Lynch Walk, 1927

CHAPTER 4

The Old Mill, Uplyme, 1927

my mother to them as walks. Once, when walking past Cathole Farm, we looked up at the granary door on the first floor and saw a row of yellow eyes gleaming in the darkness of the gap at its foot, an odd coincidence in view of the name of the farm.

Where the old Coach Road from Rookery Lane and Hodder's Corner emerges into the lane above Rocombe, there used to be the tallest gate I have ever seen. I think it was seven-barred, and it was painted white; the Six Inch Ordnance Survey Map still marks the corner as 'White Gate'. I last saw its relics in 1977, lying against the bank, but after I had described them in 1979 to John Fowles, he searched for them – in a hail-storm – and reported them gone.

Apart from very occasional outings by train or bus, we walked everywhere in early days and always carried walking-sticks. There was little traffic on the roads and horses were still in use. The forge at Uplyme stood at the angle of the road to Venlake and the main road through the village, just opposite the old Rectory which is now the Devon Hotel. One could safely play with a ball on the road. On one occasion Gulie Lister took us to tea with Miss Stanger-Leathes, then living with her invalid mother in the Stone House at Charmouth. Her young niece and nephew, Rosalie and Christopher, who were about my age, came up the Old Lyme Road with us on our way back, and we played a kind of hockey with a ball and the crooks of walking-sticks. I still possess my stick with its handle scraped and peeled by the surface of the road that evening.

Sometimes we walked to Charton Cross and along the Trinity Hill road, turning back by the lane that leads to Shapwick Grange and Cannington. At Shapwick there was a linhay with a half-wall and pillars supporting the roof. Although this linhay itself was in a farm-yard, it has always been to me the 'lonely barton by yonder coomb' of Hardy's Christmas Eve poem.

One day we were walking under the viaduct towards Uplyme when we were joined by a collie from Cannington Farm; he accompanied us nearly as far as Venlake and then turned back home. The following evening we walked past Cannington Farm in the opposite direction and the dog again came out and joined us. As he had turned back of his own accord the night before, we were not worried until we got well beyond the viaduct where the lane begins to climb towards the Sidmouth road. We then ordered him to 'Go home!' with no effect at all, even when we pretended to throw stones to discourage him. Soon afterwards, however, he disappeared into a field and we hoped we had seen the last of him, but round another turn he emerged to greet us again. Up on the main road we became seriously concerned and when we reached Ware Cross we asked a man working in his garden if he would hold the dog till we were out of reach, but he said that the animal was much too valuable for him to take any responsibility. We then tried

CHAPTER 4

Miss Gladys Stapleforth, 1928

walking down Gore Lane and when the dog had run on ahead we bolted back to the main road, but he turned and followed us, and here the situation became even worse for passing motorists began to swear at us for not keeping our dog under better control. At last we reached the police station in Hill Road, only to be told by the police, who instantly recognized him as belonging to Farmer Harris, that they could not take him in as they had one stray dog already and they thought the two would fight. They declared that we must take him back for the night to wherever we were staying; in these days of telephones and cars the situation seems unbelievable. We protested that it would be impossible to have a large dog in our upstairs sitting-room at the Royal Standard, and after much argument the police agreed that we could try to leave him in the station garden, declaring that he would certainly get out and rejoin us. So we left him in the garden and started off downhill as we could thus get away more quickly. The dog was running and barking inside the wall and I suddenly realized that the slope of the ground downhill was such that the wall was getting lower on the dog's side and that he would soon be able to jump over it. So we turned and almost ran up Hill Road with the dog still accompanying us inside the wall, but with the wall becoming a higher barrier at every step. We then dashed across to Cobb Road and down to the Royal Standard, closed the door at the foot of the stairs and climbed to the haven of our own room.

Walks, however, were usually peaceful. We often saw lizards sunning themselves on the bank beside Rhode Lane, and once we watched a field-mouse running to and fro in the sandy bank of Colway Lane. King-cups and wood anemones were always in flower in the copse of Alder Grove below the viaduct; its floor was muddy and I once emerged from it having left both my galoshes behind; my mother had to recover them with a walking-stick. At the corner of the lane nearby there still grew the mare's tails which my mother remembered from her girlhood, when her young brother called them 'cony equisetums' (like cones); they grow there still.

Another walk was through Yawl and up Knoll Hill, which is in the very heart of the valleys of Uplyme. From its smoothly curved summit we looked one evening across the Yawl valley and watched the sun setting behind Woodhouse Hill, and for the only time in my life I had the complete experience of feeling the earth swinging backwards, itself in movement while the sun was static. Knoll Hill held a mystery which seemed to be incarnate in a white owl beating the hedges of Carswell Farm below. We would make our way down to the farm and back along the lane to Uplyme church. The area was very remote in spirit, and in the quietness of the valley between Carswell Farm and Limekiln Lane there stood a vast elm tree and an ancient apple orchard; I thought of them as the Giant Elm Tree and the Magic Orchard, and when I later came to know Samuel Palmer's paintings, I felt that they had materialized straight from his canvas.

Another spot that held a mystery was a little spring of water in the deep hollow of the bank beside the lane leading from Venlake to Cannington. Further down the valley the stream which passes the cottages at Venlake was not then separated from the road by a low wall, and we once watched a cat sitting beside the stream and scooping the water with its paw; after that we always spoke of Venlake as 'the street of the fishing cat'.

We followed the round walk by Woolly and Woodhouse Hill and the area at the top of Woodhouse Lane which my mother on that early family holiday had known as Uplyme Heath. From here, taking a picnic lunch, we followed the bridle-path between moss-grown banks and overhung by trees along Trinity Hill. Where the bridle-path begins, on the hill-top above Hartgrove, there is a low twisted tree growing out of the bank. I scrambled up into the tree and looked out eastwards to Golden Cap in Dorset and then westwards to Beer Head in Devon; it linked two worlds and I have always thought of it as the tree that Drake climbed in Panama to gain a glimpse of both the Atlantic and the Pacific.

Before the war, Stonebarrow Lane was deep and rough, sunk between banks covered with primroses and violets and with a small stream running down each side; this water has long since been piped underground. We used to walk over to Charmouth and then climb the lane to the crest of Stonebarrow, picnicking among the fir trees on the western flank of the summit, looking back over Charmouth and Black Ven to Lyme. These trees constituted Cain's Folly, the word 'folly' probably being connected with the French 'feuillée' and having nothing to do with a poetic ruin. The trees are now dead, but the name remains because on the map the Ordnance Survey mistakenly printed 'Cain's Folly' where 'Fairy Dell' should be.

We sometimes used to take the bus to the top of the hill above Chideock and walk by the lane to the saddle behind Golden Cap itself, and then up to the summit. Coming back, I once enjoyed sitting and sliding down the steep inland slope from the crest, to my mother's horror when she saw the resulting state of my clothes.

There is something splendid, almost sacred, about the summit of Golden Cap; as Bennet Copplestone said, 'Upon its flat top might rest, enthroned, the gods of West Bay, or the devils'. We made the pilgrimage, walking from Lyme and back, to the ruined church of Stanton St Gabriel, this being specially poignant to me because I had read Bennet Copplestone's *The*

Treasure of Golden Cap. When I was eleven years old I had been kept indoors at Guildhall House for a day or two with a cold and my mother bought this book for me; I devoured it and I have been under its spell from that day to this. When I first acquired a camera, I concentrated on photographing as many as possible of the places in which its scenes were set.

Rain sometimes overtook our expeditions. We once walked to Lambert's Castle, and while we were eating our lunch there we watched a storm driving across Devon, a white inverted triangle of rain approaching up each valley. In those far-off days our simple picnic-basket contained starched table-napkins and we found them surprisingly effective spread out as some protection against the sheeting rain. Our shoes, however, were filled with water, and we trudged back to Lyme squelching at every step.

We once took the bus to Axminster to see the church. There was a permanent advertisement outside the station at Lyme saying that anyone spending more than five pounds at the House of Dawkins would have the railway fare refunded. We thought what fun it would be to do this, but five pounds was far outside anything that we would have spent in those days; I did eventually buy a dress at Dawkins in 1933 but it cost only a few shillings. Once or twice we went by bus to Bridport and West Bay; on one occasion it was bitterly cold and all the passengers waiting for the return bus sheltered in the Greyhound. One year we took a charabanc tour to Abbotsbury to see the swannery and the sub-tropical gardens, and we also went by train to Chard Junction and walked to Forde Abbey.

We walked once, in very early days, from Charmouth to Wootton Fitzpaine, and back by what was then unknown country to us; I remember vividly the welcome sight of the Cobb as we came down Timber Hill and realized that we had indeed found our way back to Lyme.

Every year we took the bus to Bellair and walked thence to Whitchurch Canonicorum, returning to pick up the bus at the same point. We noticed that pennies and halfpennies were placed in St Candida's shrine in the church. When my mother was old and had long since ceased to share holidays, she suffered one spring from an arthritic knee; I was in Whitchurch one day and I slipped a threepenny piece into the shrine; my mother's knee did, as it happened, begin to improve.

CHAPTER 5

Our special introduction to the natural history of Lyme came from the Lister family. In 1870 Lord Lister, his brother Arthur and a brother-in-law had together bought Highcliff as a holiday house. Lord Lister had no children but Arthur had a family of seven and the house eventually became his alone, although until 1902 Lord Lister always came there for the family Christmas and when he was elevated to the peerage in 1897 he took the title of Baron Lister of Lyme Regis. Dolly Lister gave me an ormer or abalone shell which had belonged to him; its exterior is rough and grey; the interior is iridescent blue-green. It is said that he used to sit and caress it while he was considering his medical problems.

The biographies of Lord Lister record his operating on Edward VII for appendicitis and the fact that after his coronation the King shook hands with him saying that he knew he owed his life to him. From the family we heard a story which is not, however, consistent with the published facts about the medical men involved, but which tells how when the team of consultants were called in to diagnose the King's illness just a few days before he should have been crowned, they told him that he must undergo appendicectomy and the King utterly refused. They withdrew to the window and stood in silence until the King asked why they were still there. As spokesman for the group, Lord Lister approached the bedside and said, 'We are waiting for Your Majesty to come to a more reasonable conclusion.'

Arthur Lister, F.R.S., was a member of the Society of Friends, although he was a wine merchant. His own special interest lay in botany and he was an authority on the Mycetozoa or slime-moulds, on which he wrote a monograph published by the British Museum (Natural History). He had three sons and four daughters. His eldest son was Joseph Jackson, who married Dorothea Marryat; the others were William Tindall (who became Sir William), an eminent ophthalmic surgeon, and Arthur Hugh, who married Sybil Palgrave.

Sybil was the daughter of Sir Reginald Palgrave and niece of Francis Turner Palgrave who compiled *The Golden Treasury*. Francis Turner Palgrave had bought Little Park in Haye Lane at Lyme in 1872; there he built the thatched summer-house in the garden in which, according to family tradition, he and Tennyson used to sit while they discussed poetry.

Of Arthur Lister's four daughters, Ellen ('Nell' or 'Nellie') became Mrs Phear, and the three unmarried sisters, Isabella, Gulielma and Edith, continued to live in their old home, 871 High Road, Leytonstone, Essex, while spending the summers at Highcliff until after Isabella's death in 1928. My mother stayed at Leytonstone, in a room with a powdering-closet leading out of it; she described it as a beautiful old house which had become engulfed and isolated in a very poor neighbourhood. I went to look for it in 1986 and found that it had been demolished about ten years earlier. It was near Epping Forest; the Forest, and the activities of the Essex Field Club of which she became President, played an important part in Gulielma's life. She also twice served as President of the British Mycological Society. She was the scientist among the sisters, and devoted the earlier part of her life to helping her father, especially with his *Monograph of the Mycetozoa*; she had illustrated it with her own skilful drawings and, after his death, she prepared the second edition. The name Gulielma was the feminine of Gulielmus (William), but she was always called 'Gulie', the 'G' being hard and the 'u' as in 'you', the 'Gul-' indeed being pronounced as in the heraldic term 'gules'.

Over the years she compiled a scrap-book of Lyme which is now in the Lyme Regis Museum. It is a treasure-house of local, historical and scientific information and was aptly named the *Lister Thesaurus* by Mr Wanklyn.

Gulie Lister was passionately interested in natural history and encyclopaedic in her information. She was kind and generous, but as a child I was conscious of falling far short of the standards she expected. I remember her shocked silence as she inspected a nature calendar that I was making with my own unskilful drawings. There was a collection of stuffed birds at Highcliff; she pointed out the spur on the leg of one of them and told me that there was a flower called after it; I was triumphant in then recognizing that it must be a lark. Gwen Harding was so much afraid of misidentifying flowers that she made a rule of never referring to a plant by name in Gulie's presence. On one occasion she forgot her resolution and said, quite correctly, that a certain plant was in flower. Gulie's dry comment was, 'So there's *one* flower Gwen knows, anyway.'

She took intense pleasure in all plants and I can still see the slow sweet smile breaking over her face as she stood and looked down at a patch of dog's mercury in flower on the roadside by Morgan's Grave. Once, when we were walking near Woodhouse, she took us into the Pinetum; here we met someone she knew to whom she explained that we were 'playing with the pine trees', a phrase characteristic of her but obviously perplexing to him. She took us to see *Lathraea* (toothwort) growing under a tree where the great chalk quarry is now, in what she called the Happy Valley. Many years later, when I was writing a geological paper on the Lyme valleys, I asked her the origin of the valley's name and she said that it had been given to them by friends soon after 1870 when they first came to Highcliff. Zachary Edwards, who wrote Mate's *Illustrated Lyme Regis*, published about 1902, also uses the name for the valley beyond the viaduct. I have since been told that the name Happy Valley is used in Uplyme for the other, northern, side of the viaduct, extending thence to Cuckoo Hill.

Gulie Lister had a small pocket telescope that had belonged to her friend Blanche Palmer; this she generously gave to me and it has been my constant companion in the field ever since. When I became a student of geology, she gave me a duplicate copy she possessed of the 1906 Geological Survey Memoir of *The Country near Sidmouth and Lyme Regis*; this had originally been given to Blanche Palmer by W.C. Darby, who kept the shop that is now the Toby Jug. Gulie Lister also gave me A.C.G. Cameron's book on the geology of Lyme, published by Dunster, and a photograph of the cliffs west of the town taken by Miss K. Eastment in 1896. She also gave me maps of other parts of the country, including Geikie's geological map of Scotland which has been an invaluable possession.

The eldest sister of the Lister family was Isabella, always known as 'Bella'. She too was an artist. She is remembered by her nieces as learning Greek, I think in the morning-room at Highcliff, from Mr Harding, a schoolmaster who had retired to Lyme. She was, however, much occupied with charitable work. She did much for the Cottage Hospital, and John Fowles has met someone who remembered her scrubbing floors at Rhode Hill when it was a hospital during the First World War. It was characteristic that it was she who found lodgings for us on our first visit to Lyme. I fancy that she was mainly responsible for the housekeeping at Highcliff; it was after her death in 1928 that Gulie and Edith gave up the house. Bella's death occurred while she was staying in the Pyrenees: she slipped over a precipice at Gavarnie, where she had been sketching.

Edith was the delicate one of the three and did not take part in her sisters' more robust activities, but in her the artistic talent, shared by the family, was so highly developed that painting became her main occupation. I remember her as charming and somewhat fragile-looking; Bella was less ethereal and more practical. The family was spartan, regarding creature comforts as self-indulgent. They had a family phrase, 'ruggling on', for pressing on undaunted however tired one might be.

In 1926 we were included in a party which set out to reopen an overgrown footpath through the Undercliff to Charton Bay. We actually went on hands and knees where the bushes were densest, Bella, who was over seventy, leading the way, followed by Gulie, Mr and Mrs Harding and their daughter Gwen and my mother and me. I was the only child present and I remember how kind Gwen Harding was in talking to me as we picnicked overlooking Charton Bay. On another occasion Gulie took us towards Pinhay along the cliff-top path which the Allhusen family allowed them to use.

Highcliff was built between 1811 and 1821. The dining-room was a long room on the left as you face the front door; the table used to be laid for lunch with a Dorset knob, to take the place of bread, on a folded napkin beside each place. I think the drawing-room was above the dining-room. On the ground floor, to the right as you entered, was the study, with a curved wall making it a most unusual shape. The collection of stuffed birds was kept in what must originally have been the billiard-room. The house was large and there was plenty of room for all the family activities; we envied Gulie her microscope and all her other equipment at Lyme, to which we came with only holiday luggage.

The grounds included a large kitchen-garden, in which there was a summer-house or gazebo, and there was a second gazebo on another wall to take full advantage of the view of the cliffs. Looking across to the cliffs as she stood on the lawn in front of the house, Gulie taught me the names of all the coastal features: Black Ven, Charmouth Yellow, Golden Cap, Thorncombe Beacon, Eype, Bridport Harbour, Burton Bradstock and Portland Bill. Later I learnt the more generally accepted names of some of the cliffs and in 1942 Dr Lang and I published an article in *Notes and Queries for Somerset and Dorset* in which we discussed the alternative names for them. Charmouth Yellow is Stonebarrow, while Golden Cap was sometimes known as Giltie Cup, this name being used by the family of the Listers' second gardener at Highcliff.

CHAPTER 6

Going for a row was a great excitement; one could take a boat from the Cobb and boats for hire were also drawn up on the beach between the Cobb Gate and Lucy's Jetty. In 1924 Mrs Willis treated us to a row; in 1925 we went with Mr F. Curtis in the *Bessie*, in 1926 with Mr A. Hodder in the *Mayflower* from the Cobb, and in 1927 with Mr Rattenbury in the *Boy John*. They were patient with a child's early attempts to scull. They took us along the coast towards Charmouth. I particularly enjoyed getting a view of the Buddle Bridge from the sea; in those days one could only get the view of the bridge from Coombe Street by being given access to what was then the yard of Mr Grattan's butcher's shop.

Walter Abbott was Town Crier and regularly cried through the town; from Guildhall House we listened to his voice in Cockmoil Square. In the early days he provided a means of communication of genuine town affairs; I regretted it when his cries came later to be largely advertising the cinema, and there was an incongruity between his dignified appearance and his announcement of 'Fred Astaire and Ginger Rogers in...', but his voice was as grand as ever and we were proud of his town-crying championship.

We were staying in Church Street at the time of the local elections in 1928 and children, mostly boys of eight or nine years old, marched up and down the road carrying posters and singing. Each put in the name of his own candidate:

Vote, vote, vote for Mr Woodroffe/Wiscombe/Washer,
Vote, vote, vote for Mr Woodroffe/Wiscombe/Washer,
For he is our man and we'll have him if we can,
And turn the others out of town.

Mr Rex Woodroffe, of Rhode Hill, got in by a majority of four votes over the combined votes cast for his rivals.

The Buddle Bridge, from what was then Mr Grattan's yard in Coombe Street, 1927

CHAPTER 6

An occasional feature in the streets used to be the Breton onion-sellers, with strings of onions hanging from the handlebars of their bicycles. They were picturesque figures in their dark jerseys and I invented a story for myself about smuggling in which onion-sellers played a key role, the scene of operations being the undercliffs between Lyme and Axmouth. When, long afterwards, Lady Abbot-Anderson lent me Walter Besant's *'Twas in Trafalgar's Bay*, I found something of the adventures that I had invented. It always seemed to me that the undercliffs were the ready-made scene of romantic stories, and that anyone might live rough in hiding there. I heard afterwards that in the winter of 1946–7 two German prisoners-of-war, who had escaped, lived in the undercliff for two months in a hide that they had constructed, supplying themselves by raids on Mrs Gapper's cottage, Allhallows School, Pinhay and elsewhere.

When I was a child, on holiday at Lyme, my mother's godmother used regularly to send me a postal order for half-a-crown. This was wealth to me. I acquired my first propelling pencil at the stationer's shop later run by Mrs Rolfe in Silver Street, while another year Turner's shop, next door to Guildhall House, yielded a volume of Sherlock Holmes. My mother gave me *Micah Clarke* because it was about the Monmouth Rebellion, but I was disappointed to find that it contained only one passing reference to Lyme. At Turner's shop I also occasionally and rather shamefacedly bought comics, which I never read at any other time.

To a child, the most fascinating shop was Isbell's, now the Toby Jug. Mr Isbell always had a marvellous selection of miniature toys, such as tiny dolls' rooms made in match-boxes, and other treasures. It was here, when I was nine years old, that my mother bought me a doll's high-chair to console me when I had my plait cut off; I had had a bad attack of measles the winter before and the doctor had recommended that I should have my hair cut short to strengthen its growth. I was reluctant, but less reluctant than I would otherwise have been because it was to be done at Lyme, by Miss Beer in Broad Street. Afterwards we went for a walk and before we came back into the town I was already rejoicing in the freedom of my short hair and feeling guiltily that I had no right to the toy which had been given to comfort me. I remember also a celluloid parrot on a ring-shaped perch that could be hung up, which was given me in an attempt to console me for the end of a holiday.

W.H. Smith had a small lending library at the railway station and there was a library at Dunster's at the top of Broad Street. At Dunster's too were to be found knitting wools and patterns and here I got the materials for the first cardigan I ever made. Here we also found little leather bags; Gulie Lister's pocket telescope lives in one of them to this day. Some small carved wooden brooches were on sale at one time and my mother bought two which she gave me for a subsequent birthday. I later noticed that the design of one of them seemed to be based on the motif of a roof-boss in the church at Whitchurch Canonicorum. When I was eight years old, Dunster's yielded little carved wooden birds, rather fanciful but very attractive; my mother gave me one, which I called Verity, on a day when I had confessed to a lie I had repeatedly told at home. I had the feeling that Lyme demanded integrity complete, and it was here that my mother talked to me about the importance of truth, sealing it with this little bird Verity as a sort of talisman to remind me and yet to show me that I was forgiven.

Dunster's was owned by Mr Mould. In the 1930s, when I was beginning to work on the geological history of the landslips, he still had for sale a stock of the original Dunster prints of 1840, as well as other prints and Roberts's *Account of and Guide to the Mighty Land-slip*. I bought a complete set of all five editions of Roberts's *Guide* and I undertook to arrange for them to go after my time to some library where they would be preserved as a set. I also bought a copy of Roberts's 1823 *History of Lyme-Regis*.

At Preston's shop we bought a polished ammonite, which is still a treasure on my mantlepiece. I think it was here that my mother obtained a shoe-horn made, it was said, from a red-deer antler found when the submerged forest was exposed on the beach at Charmouth in 1925. Preston's business subsequently became Aggott's the jeweller whose shop is now Richards Gifts; at Aggott's we found a little bone brooch carved into the form of a rose.

Mr Isbell was one of the chief singers in the Lyme Regis Operatic Society; in 1925 Mrs Case's daughter Nellie was singing in the chorus of *The Yeomen of the Guard* and my mother took me to see it as my first introduction to opera. The performance was in the Drill Hall, now the Marine Theatre, and it was very good. Mr Isbell took the part of Jack Point and we both thought that he was far better than Henry Lytton whom we later saw in the same role in a performance by the D'Oyly Carte Opera Company itself. The following year Mr Isbell was taking the part of the Lord High Executioner in *The Mikado*. There is a reference in this opera to Knightsbridge and at Lyme the name Combpyne had been substituted for it, to a roar of delight from the audience. I was surprised and impressed that Gilbert should have known of Combpyne and referred to it thus, and my mother had to explain to me that it was a gag, a totally new concept to me.

I enjoyed the *The Mikado*, but the opera had none of the deeply moving quality of *The Yeomen of the Guard*. Blended with 'I have a song to sing, O!' was the sound of waves breaking on the sea-wall outside, and when we came out we saw what I described to myself as 'the red Cobb light gleaming over the water'. Banal as this phrase was, it was my own and to this day I never see that light without thinking of it. One evening, after our return home, I remember my mother running upstairs to tell me that our next-door neighbour was playing 'I have a song to sing, O!', which to me conjured up the sight and sound of Lyme's sea-walls. My mother gave me the score of the opera so that I could pick out the tune for myself on the piano. Twenty-five years later I was in Lyme when *The Yeomen* was again being performed and, after much hesitation over the risk of trying to recapture the joy, I decided to go. I met Mr Isbell in Bridge Street and told him that I had heard him sing Jack Point in that earlier performance; to my amazement and delight he said that he was singing it again as well as producing the opera. I went in eager but anxious anticipation; fortunately, the performance carried all the same magic as the earlier memory.

CHAPTER 7

In 1923, on a wet day, my mother took me to the Drill Hall to see a 'Pageant of Children in Fiction', including characters from *The Water Babies, Alice in Wonderland, The Rose and the Ring, Nicholas Nickleby* and other books. This was given in aid of the Waifs and Strays.

In general, however, we had no external entertainment on our holidays. In the evening, following family tradition, my mother read the Waverley Novels aloud to me; the first of these was *The Talisman*, which we finished at Lyme in 1924. I shall always associate *The Monastery* with the sitting-room at Guildhall House.

I had a red toy wooden boat called the *Nymph* which did not balance well, but Mrs Case's son, Bert, most kindly trimmed it for me so that it sailed perfectly. Later I had another boat, of polished wood, which I called *The Wild Swan of Lyme Regis*, after I had read *The Treasure of Golden Cap*.

We spent much time at the Cobb. In those days the lobster-pots were all made of withies and the boats were built of wood, for fibreglass and plastic were of course unknown. The sound of the Cobb was quite different: the ropes made a quiet flapping against the wooden masts, unlike the metallic ring of wire stays on the hollow aluminium masts of today. The level of the sand in the harbour used to be much lower than it is now and one had to climb a ladder to the North Wall; but then, as now, sandpipers frequented the beach behind the buildings. We used to sit on the benches in the fishermen's open shelters, where Anita and I 'played at houses' the year that she was there too. My mother introduced me to the Whispering Gallery effect along the High Wall between the Gin Shop and Granny's Teeth; she had known of this on her early holiday as a girl.

I was fond of going by myself down the Gun Cliff steps and sitting on the sloping face above the base of the sea-wall, watching the sand-hoppers and generally contemplating. Later on,

CHAPTER 7

The Cobb, 1927

when I read Binyon's 'Tristram's End', it was the Gun Cliff that I pictured to myself in the description of Iseult gazing up to Tristram by 'the rusted rail And rock-hewn steps'.

As a child, I used to dig sand-castles on the beach near Lucy's Jetty and make channels for the little outflows of water that issued from under the Parade. I called the river-system that I thus made a 'riviera' and I was puzzled when my mother said that this was not what the word meant. I was fascinated by the gush of water from the bank on the west side of Roman Road and when, more than thirty years later, I was asked by the Southern Region of British Rail to write a report on the subsidence of Lyme station, I considered the problem at home before I came to Lyme to do the field-work, and suddenly remembered the flow of water nearby that had so enchanted me as a child. I thought I might have found the key to the subsidence and when I came to investigate and map the station site it proved indeed to be the source of the trouble.

On the other side of the main road, Clappentail House had, in early days, in the seaward side of the bay-window, a pane of old glass which reflected the light with rainbow iridescence. Further down the road, a window at Kent House was always filled with cacti in pots and with little texts; I called these 'texts and caxters', using the word by which our 'help' used to speak of my cacti at home.

In the stone garden wall of St Andrew's and the adjacent houses in Silver Street, one of the blocks of chert has a hollow in it, just large enough to take two finger-tips. This fascinated me and I remember poking moss and a celandine flower into it, almost as an offering to the god of such mysteries.

Tennyson's 'Crossing the Bar' has always seemed to describe the high tide 'too full for sound or foam' against the sea-wall just before one comes to the Cobb hamlet. Looking here at the moonlight on the sea I once wrote in my diary that it gave one the feeling that one could slip over the world's end. However, the heart of Lyme lay to me at the Cobb Gate. In an anthology that I had as a child, I found a poem by Nora Holland about gulls:

Spirits of old mariners...
Drake's and Hawkins' buccaneers,
So do seamen say,

and I pictured these at the Cobb Gate; it was only in recent years that I heard of the legend in Burton Bradstock that the men who have gone become gulls. When I read Newbolt's poems, the line 'Hear what the sea-wind saith' again conjured up the Cobb Gate to me, and it was here too that I thought of Longfellow's

"Wouldst thou," — so the helmsman answered, —
"Learn the secret of the sea?"

'The secret of the sea' seemed to me to be the ultimate mystery, and it was held at the Cobb Gate.

CHAPTER 8

Mrs Goldsworthy, with whom we had stayed in Marine Parade, later moved to Coombe Street. Here her bedroom window looked across to the church tower, and she told us that she took comfort from its reminder of 'the promise'.

We ourselves always spent much time looking at the church. The organ used to be in the south chapel of the chancel and above it was the angel, playing a wind instrument, which is now over the south doorway. In the gallery was the tapestry which had been presented by the Reverend Edward Peek in 1886; it was made about 1510 and showed the scene of a marriage which may have been that of Catherine of Aragon either to Prince Arthur or subsequently to Henry VIII. This tapestry was later hung in the nave and I got to know its figures so well that when it was handed over to the National Trust in 1977, to be hung at Trerice in Cornwall, I felt as if I had been parted from old friends whom I should probably never see again. I always looked long at the windows, especially at the War Memorial. Then there was the old lectern containing the 'Bad' Bible, the chained 'Breeches Bible', and Erasmus's Paraphrase of the Gospel of St Luke. There was the pulpit with its inscription 'To God's Glory Richard Harvey of London Mercer and Marchant Adventurer 1613 Faith is by Hearing', and William Dare's initials were carved on the capital of a pillar. I was most touched in 1948 to be admitted to the locked gallery by a churchwarden because I had known the Lister family; the next Sunday at morning service he gave me a seat in the otherwise unoccupied Corporation pew, which was a memorable experience.

When I was teaching at the King's School at Ely, I coached a sixth form boy, Angus Cowan, for Sandhurst, and I asked him one day why he was studying the map of Devon in his atlas. He said that he was looking for Seaton because his mother's family had come from somewhere near there; I enquired the name and he said that I should not know it, it was a little place called

Lyme Regis. He added that his family had built part of the church there; this sounded to me improbable, but I asked what his mother's maiden name had been. He replied, 'Hassard'. I said, '"John Hassard built this to the glorie of almightie God in the eightieth yeare of his age Anno Domini 1611."' The boy stared. 'You *know* it,' he said, 'I'm descended from him.'

It is the shore below Long Entry that I picture to myself in Tennyson's 'Break, break, break, On thy cold grey stones, O Sea!'. The beach beyond the Church Cliffs jetty was reckoned the great place for fossil-collecting; indeed we spoke of it as the Fossil Beach. In 1923, when it was approached by a rough muddy scramble, we were taken along there in search of fossils by Sidney ('Dick') Curtis, who had been the last owner of the old Fossil Depot in Bridge Street, before its demolition in 1913. He found us ammonites and an ichthyosaur vertebra that was my special treasure. He told us the history of his family; he was one of the twenty-three children who had been born in the cottage on Church Cliffs of which Channel View is an enlarged and rebuilt descendant. Thirteen of them grew up; it was Sam Curtis who used to sit on a chair, smoking his pipe on the pavement outside his bow-windowed cottage just below the London Inn in Church Street. The bow-window has since been removed and, with present-day traffic, no one who sat on the pavement would long survive. Sidney Curtis died in 1928. He had a little grand-daughter whose parents lived at 55 Church Street; she took great pleasure in the dolls that I brought with me in a basket and that I kept on the wide ledge inside our sitting-room window, so we gave her a doll. Gulie Lister told us that, according to the church registers, the family were originally called Cortez and were believed to be descended from a Spaniard wrecked in the Armada.

In 1948, when one of the next generation, Joe Curtis, was living on Church Cliffs, he told me that he was suing the County Council for the right, enjoyed by his family for 120 years, to draw up their boats on the beach between the Gun Cliff and Church Cliff jetty. He said that this beach was traditionally called Curtis Cove or Bears' Creek, as 'they always call us the Sea-bears in Lyme, because the Curtises are always in and out of the water'.

In 1934 we met Mr Hann, another man who collected fossils. He sold them for what was in those days a rather high price, but his finds had the great advantage of having their provenance accurately recorded.

My first introduction to Ecclesiastes came at Lyme. We were walking past the church, one day when I was a child, and a coffin was being carried into a house in Monmouth Street. An old man who was passing called to another blue-jerseyed seaman, 'Someone gone to his long

Winter's Farm, Rocombe, 1927: *it was later destroyed by fire*

CHAPTER 8

home'. I asked my mother what this meant and she explained, adding that she had hoped that I had not noticed the coffin. I had seen it, but I was not disturbed; there was something elemental about the old man's comment.

The only shadow over my joy in Lyme used to be my fear of fire. When I was four years old, Gray's factory in Cambridge, where cricket bats were made, was burnt out; it was just at the other side of the lane from the end of our garden. I was held up to see the fire at its height, when the roof had fallen in, and it was a sight that has haunted me ever since. My nurse, moreover, had a horror of thatch, which she instilled into me. In 1924, when Mrs Willis and Anita were staying in Lyme, we all went one day for a walk through Uplyme, and Anita and I were playing the game of each thinking of a word and the other having to find out by questioning what the word was. We were passing Mona House, the two-storey back part of which was then thatched, and this made me think at once of 'fire-engine' as the word for Anita to try to discover. A day or two later we passed the house again, and it was with a violent shock and almost with a sense of second-sight that I saw that the thatched part had been burnt down and the rest severely damaged. Mr Stapleforth, from the Black Dog Inn, had rescued Lady Jones by ladder from her bedroom with the bay-window. We walked on by Limekiln Lane and there we came to the shell of another house which Mrs Case later told us had been burnt out since Christmas. There was a small daytime fire in Coombe Street while we were staying in Guildhall House, and I remember hearing an old fisherman saying, 'It isn't going to be much'. Over the years I heard of other fires in and near Lyme, including that at Berne Farm, the home of Sir George Somers, and Winter's Farm at Rocombe.

CHAPTER 9

We scarcely ever came to Lyme without unexpectedly meeting someone from Cambridge. In 1923 Miss A.B. Collier, a mathematician and Vice-Principal of Newnham, was staying at Argyle House; in 1924 Miss M.H. Wood, then Principal of the Cambridge Training College for Women (now Hughes Hall), had taken one of the Lymbrook Cottages with a friend; in 1928 we met Miss E.E.H. Welsford, then lecturer in English at Newnham. It must have been in 1925 that, on our first evening, as we climbed to the seat on the Knap in the Holmbush Fields, we met Miss J.P. Strachey, then Principal of Newnham, coming down from it with her brother, Lytton Strachey, to whom she introduced us.

Once we looked up at the window of Bay Cottage, half expecting to see Jane Austen, to meet instead the beaming smile of our local dairy-man, who was there with his wife convalescing after an illness. One year we went to see a Cambridge family who were in lodgings in Cobb Road, and on another occasion friends of my mother's were staying at Glenholme. A visitor with whom we had no personal connection was Mrs (later Dame Mary) Scharlieb, the pioneer of women entering the medical profession, who was staying across the road at Guildhall Cottage – or so I believe, though I have no written record of this.

In 1923 Mrs Monkhouse and her daughter Bella, who were old friends of my mother's family, were staying at the Royal Standard and we went to tea with them in the lovely upstairs sitting-room overlooking the Cobb. Eventually, in 1934, we took these rooms ourselves. We were certain that when Captain Benwick moved out of the Harvilles' house, so that they could nurse Louisa Musgrove, he slept instead at the Royal Standard.

Mrs Grattan was one of the ten daughters of Frank Hitchcock, second gardener at Highcliff; about 1900 she married the licensee of the Royal Standard and she continued to run the inn single-handed for eleven years after his early death, until her marriage with Mr Grattan, the

CHAPTER 9

The Cobb hamlet, 1932: *the house to the right is Cobb Cliff; that next to it is Wings, behind Wings is the Chalet; all have now gone*

Damage to Marine Parade, 1927

butcher. Mr Grattan's brother Freddie also came to live at the inn, having a little room at the front of the ground floor. At the back was the bar, always known as 'the men's kitchen', picturesque with a settle and a spittoon. We never heard a sound from the men's kitchen, although it was underneath our room. The inn was very quiet and Mrs Grattan firmly locked the door if she saw anyone approaching who she thought might be 'drinky'. We were always the first spring visitors and Mrs Grattan did a great redecorating before our arrival, including repainting the sponge-bath which had come from Highcliff.

As in our earlier Lyme lodgings, we bought our own food, and Mrs Grattan cooked it for us; we used to order our groceries from Mr Foxwell, in what is now the Fossil Shop in Bridge Street, and later from Ralph K. Brewer (where Hartley's is now) in Broad Street; the things used to be sent by cart along the cart-road and then across the sand at low tide. In the 1920s fresh fish was sold from Beer boats which were drawn up on the beach between the Cobb Gate and Lucy's Jetty, but by the 1930s this had ceased.

The new Cobb Arms was built in 1937; before that, the slate-hung building above the old Watch House in Cobb Road was the inn. Opposite it was the harbour-master's house, which still had its portico, below the pediment, with a red lamp. The old lifeboat house, burnt down in 1935, stood next to the Cobb on the west side. Along the Parade, Wings and Cobb Cliff were still standing, but the land was already liable to slip and the Parade was occasionally broken.

Mrs Grattan always spoke of living 'up Cobb'. She had a phrase, 'to have a crave', which meant to have some occupation on which one's heart was set; I remember her watching a man painting a boat and saying, 'Ah, he's got a crave'. She had the lovely old speech with prolonged vowels and always spoke of the 'Carparation' and 'Tarquay'.

The peace of sitting reading, writing or painting in the big bow-window overlooking the Cobb was one of the most fruitful experiences. I still have, in my sitting-room at Cambridge, a framed water-colour of that quiet view which I painted in 1934. Whenever I think of St Augustine and his mother Monica looking over the sea, I picture them in that window of the Royal Standard.

From this vantage-point we watched the sailing vessels that brought cement from the Isle of Wight to the Cobb for Axminster; I made drawings in my sketch-book of most of these boats. We had already seen, in 1932, the *Maggie Annie* of Barnstaple. In April 1934 there was the *Mary Eliezer*, and in March 1935 the *Lady Daphne* of Rochester with her beautiful carving; in the evening her rigging was silhouetted against the sky with Venus hanging above. When she first came into the harbour she was too low in the water and she had to be turned and taken to

The *Maggie Annie* of
Barnstaple, 1932

CHAPTER 9

The *Lady Daphne* of Rochester, 1935
(Drawn by the author.)

Victoria Pier; as she was turned, under the direction of the harbour-master, she filled the whole width of the harbour entrance. The manoeuvre was achieved by muscular power, using poles and ropes. This was on a Thursday and she sailed again the following Monday.

In April 1937 the *Lady Jean* of Rochester came in, sister ship to the *Lady Daphne* and with similar carving. In March 1938 the *Seine* of Rochester was in the Cobb, and in April the *Hanna* of Poole; the *Hanna* was there again in March 1939.

While we were up Cobb, we went in 1935 to see Dr Lumsden about some minor ailment. He lived at Springfield and I remember the force of the wind blowing up Woodmead Road each time we rang the doorbell till we found him at home. He was most helpful and we had a delightful little talk with him in his family surroundings.

That same year we went to Sir Maurice Abbot-Anderson's house, to sign a petition against the development of shops on the sea-front. Four years later I went to an open meeting of the Lyme Regis Preservation Society at which Major Ormsby Allhusen was in the chair. This gave me the chance of thanking him personally for the permission he had kindly given me by letter to go through the grounds of Pinhay in order to examine the landslipped Chapel Rocks.

The *Hanna* of Poole, 1939
(Drawn by the author.)

CHAPTER 10

The sitting-room at the Royal Standard was where, on 1 January 1915, Mr and Mrs Harding and Gwen had supper with their friends, the Patterson family, who were staying there, and where they heard the news of the loss of the *Formidable*. Their departure was delayed to allow the Pattersons' son to show his lantern-slides, so it was late when they returned home, choosing to go along the Parade as the storm which had raged all day had now subsided. This series of chances led to Gwen Harding, with her exceptionally keen eyesight, being at the Cobb Gate when the boat with the *Formidable* survivors was approaching land; she detected it in the darkness and refused to move until she had convinced her parents that it was there. They then roused the police and all the neighbourhood to come to the rescue of the men; the dead were taken into the cinema, in what had been the old Assembly Rooms at Cobb Gate. I used to visit Gwen in her old age, when she sat by the fire at Churnside in Hill Rise, looking picturesque with her white hair and her blue velvet jacket, telling again the epic story of that night long ago. Until she became too arthritic and infirm, she took a wreath every year to the *Formidable* grave in the cemetery.

Mr Harding was much interested in the history of Lyme and discussed it with Cyril Wanklyn. Gwen remembered how she used to be sent as a runner carrying messages between Churnside and Timber Hill, where Mr Wanklyn lived at Overton, now renamed Treetops. He published the first edition of *Lyme Regis, a retrospect* in 1922, and the second edition in 1927. I was by then passionately interested in the history of Lyme and my mother gave me a copy of the new edition; she obtained it from Mr Walter Hardy of St Michael's Hotel, who held the stock. We then got into correspondence with Mr Wanklyn. He published his later material largely in the form of articles in *Pulman's Weekly News*; as each of these appeared, he used to send me an offprint; I would study it and write to him discussing it, and he would reply, usually on a closely written and almost illegible postcard. He prepared a reprint of these articles and it was published in 1944, after his death, as the volume *Lyme Leaflets*; his family generously gave copies to his friends.

His major work was elucidating the municipal documents of the town from the early fourteenth century onwards. After he had unearthed them, he had them transcribed at the Record Office. He then indexed them and completed the series of over eighty volumes which were at first kept in Lyme Museum but are now in the Dorset County Record Office.

His methods were idiosyncratic, partly no doubt as a result of his almost total deafness. He lived alone in what I felt to be a rather pathetic state of isolation, but he came into the town by bus with his small white dog which he called Jane Austen. It was many years before I met him, but on my visits to Lyme in 1940 and 1942 he invited me to tea and we sat in what had been built as the music-room of the house. He had an ear-trumpet and it was possible to make him hear, but he was sadly conscious of his infirmity and of its effect on him.

He did much work for the historical side of the Museum, while the geological side was in the hands of Dr Wyatt Wingrave. He too was totally deaf; he had been a distinguished medical man, specializing in throat and ear problems, but he had lost his hearing through diphtheria caught, so we were told, from one of his patients. After he retired to Lyme he set up the Museum and he used to give lectures, or demonstrations as he called them. I remember as a child hearing the strange sounds that he made to himself without knowing it as he came up the stairs. He carried a tablet and pencil and we wrote down our side of the conversation; he was very quick at recognizing what other people were about to say. When I heard him lecture in 1923, he had been investigating the spiral curvature of shells, dextral or sinistral, and he talked about this, pointing out that spiral staircases were built in dextral form so that the defender would be free to use his sword-arm while the attacker would be hampered by the newel of the stair. I am afraid that this is all I remember of my earliest geological lecture.

He lived in the house called Cobbe, which is now the Harbour Inn; in his later years he became an invalid and he was invested with the Freedom of Lyme Regis in his own house. One of his daughters lived in a charming old house in Mill Green, but she has now died.

Dr Wyatt Wingrave's geological correspondence has been preserved in the Museum, and I am grateful to John Fowles, the Curator, for allowing me to see it; it reveals Dr Wingrave as having a wide circle of friends with whom he discussed local problems. The collection includes a letter from Dr W.D. Lang, explaining how he needed a complete sequence of ammonites in order to study their evolution, and therefore he was going to collect them inch by inch from the Charmouth cliffs. This is evidently what led him to his classic mapping of the cliffs, dividing the Lower Lias into 138 beds, which was published in the *Proceedings of the Geologists' Association* for 1914.

W.D. Lang was a member of the staff of the Department of Geology at the British Museum (Natural History), being appointed Keeper of Geology in 1928, and elected F.R.S. in 1929. He had family connections with Dorset, and a holiday spent in Charmouth in 1898 determined much of the future course of his life. He was greatly attracted to the village, the cliffs and the Vale of Marshwood, and he met Miss Georgiana ('Nina') Dixon whom he married in 1908. From the time of his first visit onwards he spent most of his holidays in Charmouth, finally retiring in 1938 to the house which he built in Lower Sea Lane, where he lived until his death in 1966. He named the house Lias Lea; to its north lay the orchard which they called the Norton. After Dr Lang's death, Mrs Lang and their daughter, Brenda, moved into a bungalow which they had built in the Norton. They transferred the name Lias Lea to this bungalow, which is approached from Higher Sea Lane, and the house in Lower Sea Lane was renamed Honeywood by its new owners.

Dr Lang had suffered from heart strain in boyhood and as a result he concentrated all his energies on a limited area within walking distance of Charmouth. His knowledge of the cliffs and of the Vale of Marshwood was encyclopaedic, and embraced the stratigraphy and palaeontology, the history of the landscape, and the present-day flora and fauna. He had outstanding powers of observation and found it difficult to believe that other people did not share his knowledge. In my youthful ignorance, I was once uncertain as to whether or not some birds that I had seen over Golden Cap could have been buzzards. When I asked him about this, his anxious reply was, 'Is there something wrong with your eyesight, then?' To walk along the beach with him was a memorable experience; he would pick up fossils and fragments of rock and say instantly from which of the 138 beds they had fallen. One April day in 1942, the cliff happened to be dry and relatively easily scaled, and he cast a longing eye up it and said, 'Shall we go up?' We climbed it and explored Black Ven *sensu stricto*, the 'black bog' which gives the cliff its name and which is seldom accessible; he had not been there for twenty years.

Dr Lang served as President of the Dorset Natural History and Archaeological Society from 1938 to 1940; he was subsequently a member of the Council and he was Vice-President from 1956 until his death. For many years he was responsible for the Society's 'Geological Notes'

This group, taken by Mrs Lang at the foot of the Church Cliffs at Lyme in 1915, shows from left to right: W.D. Lang, Gulie Lister, Geoffrey Lang (son of Dr Lang), Gwen Harding and her father W.G. Harding.
The original of this photograph, which is reproduced by kind permission of Dr Lang's daughter Brenda, is annotated by Dr Lang with the quarrymen's names for the Blue Lias limestone beds shown in the background.

and other records of natural history, and he published many papers in its *Proceedings*. A number of these dealt with Mary Anning in whom he was especially interested, and he made many discoveries about her and her circle.

In his retirement, Dr Lang never, so far as I know, left Charmouth for a holiday, except when he and Mrs Lang stayed once or twice at Underhill Farm in the Ware Cliffs beyond Lyme. He was essentially a man of Dorset, and Devon had comparatively little appeal for him. In spite of his interest in Mary Anning he belonged to Charmouth and not to Lyme, but in the early years of his retirement he did invaluable work, primarily in the field of natural history, for the Philpot Museum, as the Lyme Regis Museum was then called. He was not much interested in history, apart from that of geology, and he told me that he had thrown away the nails from the scaffold on which the Monmouth rebels had been hanged, because he considered them 'morbid'. How often had I gazed at them with reverence and with a sense of immediacy. Nor did he care for Hardy, but his great literary love was for Horace and Milton. He wrote long fascinating letters, in an exquisite hand and full of interesting and entertaining observations on everything that had come his way.

In 1948 the Philpot Museum was in a very bad state, with its exhibits in a chaotic condition, and Dr Lang resigned from the Trustees because he felt the situation to be hopeless. Mr Geake and Mr Tattersall had been Curators until 1946, but from then until 1960 there was no Curator. Mr Marshall was appointed in 1960 and Mr Bucknall in 1964; when Mr E.S. Gosling took charge in 1965 he put a vigorous effort into restoring the Museum, and in particular into saving the pictures that were being ruined by damp in the salt-impregnated walls.

CHAPTER 11

The decay of the Museum was at least in part a consequence of the Second World War, when Lyme was perhaps more changed than is generally realized because no photographs of harbours or military installations were allowed, and no descriptions were published. I saw it in 1940, 1942 and 1945, but in 1944 it was not possible to visit it in the spring as access to the coast was prohibited and all non-residents were obliged to leave.

By 1942 there were concrete fortifications at the Cobb Gate and on Lucy's Jetty. All along Marine Parade the railings carried stakes seven feet high supporting curtains of barbed wire through which the sea was almost invisible. One or two approaches to the beach were tunnelled through it, but I thought it was not advisable to go on to the beach because of the risk of stray mines. One was not allowed to go along the Parade after sunset without a permit. The beach behind the Royal Standard was covered with concrete and barbed wire. The Cobb itself was entirely cut off. It was covered with what I described in a letter as 'an almost incredibly colossal defence of iron girders and barbed wire'; it was festooned all over with wire entanglements and there were concrete pill-boxes.

A coastal battery was installed in Rhodehorn Plantation; the remains of foundations and of a fireplace and chimney are still to be found there beside the old coach road and beside the left-hand path where the cliff recedes beyond the Plantation. There was an impressive coastal patrol. It was rumoured, but I do not know how truly, that a flare from an aeroplane caused the fire at the house called Maries in Pine Walk in April 1942.

I carried round with me the leaflet listing subjects which one was forbidden to photograph and I obeyed it scrupulously, but I had no intention of allowing a war to interfere with my observations on the landslips and I thought it prudent to make myself and my object known before I was accused of suspicious behaviour. So on my first morning at Lyme in 1940 I went to the police station and asked how I could report my presence to the Commanding Officer; the police did not know, but they took my name and address themselves. When I returned to the hotel I found that a policeman had called with a form for me to fill in; I duly completed it and took it back to the police station but there they said that they did not want it. I had no further trouble, but I had a distinct impression in the hotel that I was felt to have lowered the tone of the establishment.

A few days later a Scottish regiment, complete with bagpipes, arrived in the town and suddenly the streets were filled with Scots voices as the men hung out of upper windows and propped up every lamp-post and door-post. I heard a column singing 'Loch Lomond' and 'Annie Laurie' to the accompaniment of a mouth-organ as they marched down Charmouth Road.

By 1942 no bombs had fallen but there were frequent air raid 'alerts'; in one fortnight in April I experienced seven alerts in Lyme and four in Charmouth. Lyme was controlled from Exeter and Charmouth from Southampton, so one might be peaceful while the other was having an alert. Dr and Mrs Lang were active in Air Raid Precautions ('A.R.P.') and whenever I went to see them after the Lyme siren had wailed I had to find out as soon as I reached Charmouth whether or not the village whistle had sounded, for, if it had, Dr and Mrs Lang would be out on their duties.

In 1942 Dr Lang was told by the Commanding Officer at Charmouth that there was no danger on the shore there except from soldiers practising throwing hand-grenades over the cliffs, and he would see that they were otherwise occupied any morning that Dr Lang chose to take me out for geological purposes. However, on the day on which we made our way through the wire to the beach and then climbed into Black Ven itself, he had, so far as I know, given no warning to the military authorities and I was relieved when we reached the village again. I think it is likely that the grenade-throwing was done on Stonebarrow rather than on Black Ven; there was a radio-location hut there, and the soldiers made a vain attempt to reach water by digging a well in the Upper Greensand on the summit.

In the undercliff in 1945, I met a gang of Italians from the prisoner-of-war camp at Seaton, doing some work with wire near Charton Goyle under the guard of a British sergeant. One of them settled down to talk to me and asked to walk back to Lyme with me. I pretended that I had friends waiting for me and, telling him that he could not come, I set off back towards Lyme. The sergeant was sitting beside the path to see that no prisoners went beyond that point, and I was relieved to see him and to hear his cheerful greeting, 'Gosh, isn't it hot?'

By 1945 it was possible to go along the Cobb again, except for the part by the buildings. There was still a pill-box by the Gin Shop and one at the far end of the Cobb. All trace of the wartime defences has now disappeared so completely that it is difficult to remember them and I have taken these descriptions from my own diaries and letters.

CHAPTER 12

As the years go by, Lyme changes; the town grows, the cliffs fall into the sea and footpaths disappear, and yet it remains the same. My mother, looking at the view from the Knap, used to quote:

Age cannot wither her, nor custom stale
Her infinite variety.

When I was nine years old I began to write a book about Lyme. It had a handsome title page with the Borough coat of arms (involving the delight of silver paint with its special smell); a frontispiece (a painting, done from memory, of the cliffs seen from the Knap); a dedication to my mother and Dolly Lister; an ambitious table of contents; a plan of the town (drawn from memory as I had no map); and the first two chapters. Although it never got any further, I always wanted to write it.

As I grew older, the desire to express my feelings about Lyme became stronger and stronger; I could not paint well enough and I never managed to write much poetry about Lyme itself, but at last geology opened the way. As a member of the Sedgwick Club at Cambridge, I had to read a geological paper and the landslips were the obvious subject. It was then approaching the centenary of the 1839 slip at Dowlands, so I wrote articles for *Country Life* and for *Notes and Queries for Somerset and Dorset*. I also wrote a paper on the coastal landslips of south-east Devon for the *Proceedings of the Geologists' Association* in 1940, followed in 1941 by a paper on the coastal landslips of west Dorset, and in 1946 by an examination of the valley-system of Lyme Regis. A third of a century after my first paper, I had to provide a presidential address for the Geologists' Association, and in 'Landslips near Lyme Regis' I brought my study up to date in 1973; this has since been reprinted as a separate booklet by Serendip Books at Lyme.

To use Mrs Grattan's phrase, I have a crave where Lyme is concerned. The place has been so integral to my life that it has informed many of my ideas. Eventually, in one instance, there proved to be a true connection between imagination and reality. In early days, on the Lymeward journey every spring, the sight of the lion on the Lambeth brewery meant that Waterloo was near, so that the lion to me seemed a harbinger of Lyme. When the site of the brewery was cleared for the building of the Royal Festival Hall, the lion was transferred to the end of Westminster Bridge and investigation then revealed that he was made of Coade Stone. The Coade family who made the stone were closely associated with Lyme and so the lion was indeed a link with the town.

INDEX

Page numbers in italic refer to illustrations.

Abbott, Walter (town crier)   39
Alder Grove   12, 32
Allhallows School   23, 41
Ames's Wall, Pinhay   23
Anemones, Wood   32
Arber, Agnes (mother)   4–6, 21, *26*
Arber, Professor Edward (grandfather)   4
Arber, Newell (father)   4–5
Assembly Rooms   14, *18*, 59
Axminster-Lyme railway   12

Bell Cliff Boarding House (Mrs Pocock)   9
Black Dog Inn   27, 51
Black Ven   21, 33, 38, 61, 65
Brazil, Angela   9
Bridge Street   6, 7, *8*, 49, 55
Broad Street   14, *15*, *19*, 41, 55
Buddle Bridge   39, *40*

Cain's Folly   33
Cameron, A.C.G.   37

Cannington   12, 27, 30, 33
Case family   6, 7, *8*, 9
Cathole Farm   27, 30
Cedar Cottage, East Cliff   9
Cement boats   55, *56*, 57, *57*, 58
Charmouth footpath   11, 21
Charmouth Road   14, 21, 27
Church, Lyme Regis   48–9
Church Street   7, *9*, *10*, 49
Coastal features   38
Cobb   2, 34, 39, 44, *45*, 52, *53*, 55, *56*, *57*, *58*, 64, 66
Cobb Gate   14, *18*, 39, 46–7, 55, 59, 64
Cobb Road   55
Cockmoil Square   7, 39
Combpyne station   12, 23
Coombe Street   2, *16*, 27, 39, 48
Copplestone, Bennet (*Treasure of Golden Cap*)   33–4
Cumberland Cottage   14
Curtis family   49

Daisies (hen-and-chicken)   21

Dawkins, House of (Axminster) 34
Devil's Bellows 21
Devon Hotel (old rectory) 30
Dog's mercury 37
Donkey Green 22
Dowlands Farm 23, 27
Drill Hall (now Marine Theatre) 42, 44
Dunster's 41–2

Edward VII 35
Edwards, Zachary 37
Fairfield 14
Fires at Lyme 51
Forge (Lyme Regis) 14
Forge (Uplyme) 30
Formidable, H.M.S. 59
'Fossil Beach' 49
Freeman House (now Marlray) 9, *10*
Frost's Corner 14

Gapper, Mrs 23
    Cottage of *24*, 41
Geological Survey Memoir, 1906: *The Country near Sidmouth and Lyme Regis* 37
Giant's Grave 22–3
Goat Island 23, 27
Golden Cap 33, 38, 61
Gosling Bridge 2, 27
Govier, Ada 7
Govier, Samuel (master smith) 7, 14

Grattan, Mrs 52, 55
Guildhall House 6, 7, *8*, 9

Happy Valley 37
Harding, Gwen 36, 38, 59, *62*
Harding, W.G. 37, 38, 59, *62*
Hassard, John 49
Haye Lane 14, 27, 36
Highcliff (Listers' home) 5, 35, 36, 37, 38, 52, 55
Holmbush Fields 22, 52
Horn Bridge 27

Isbell, Mr 42, 43
Isbell's shop (now Toby Jug) 9, 41

Jessie Norcross (sailing vessel) 20

King-cups 12, 32
Kipling, Rudyard 5
Knap 22, 52, 67
Knoll Hill 32

Landslip 1, 23, 27
Lang, Dr W.D. 38, 60–63, *62*, 65
Langmoor Cottage 14
Lepers' Well 27
Lifeboat (*Thomas Masterman Hardy*) 20
Lister family 35
    Arthur 2, 35–6
    Dorothea (Dolly) 4, 5–6, 35
    Edith 36, 37–8

INDEX

Gulielma (Gulie)   2, 4, 5, 27, 30, 36–7, 38, 49, *62*
Isabella (Bella)   6, 36, 37-8
Joseph Jackson   4, 35
Lord   35
'Lister Thesaurus'   36
Little Cliff (now Upper Cobb)   14
Little Park   36
London Inn   14, 49
Lynch Walk   27, *28*

Mare's tails   32
Marine Parade   9, *17*, 46, 48, *54*, 55, 64
Marryat, Dorothea
   See Lister, Dorothea
Mona House   51
Morgan's Grave   37
Museum, Lyme (Philpot)   7, 60–61, 63, 64
Mycetozoa   2, 35, 36

Neill, A.S.   27

Operatic Society, Lyme Regis   7, 42–3

Palgrave
   F.T.   36
   Sybil   35–6
Pine Walk   14, 22, 64
Pinhay   23, 38, 41, 57
Pocock, Mrs   9
Pound Street   14

Prisoners-of-war
   German   41
   Italian   65

Rhode Hill   37, 39
Rhodehorn Plantation   21, 64
Roberts, George (schoolmaster)   14
   Account of and Guide to the Mighty Landslip (1840)   42
   History of Lyme-Regis (1823)   42
Robertson, Agnes Lucy (grandmother)   1, 2
Robertson, Henry Robert (grandfather)   2
Robertson, Janet (aunt)   2, 3, 9, 12
Rousdon (now Allhallows School)   23
Royal Standard   9, 52, 55, 59, 64

Salisbury   11–12
Siege of Lyme   14
Shapwick Grange   12, 30
Sidmouth Road   14
Silver Street   6, 41, 46
Spittles   21
Stanton St Gabriel   33
Station (Lyme railway)   41, 46
Stonebarrow   33, 38, 65
   Lane   33
Summerhill   14, 27

Toby Jug (once Darby's, later Isbell's, shop)   9, 37, 41
Toothwort   37
Tudbold Almshouses   14

Turner, Agnes Lucy
  See Robertson, Agnes Lucy
Turner, Benjamin Brecknell (great-grandfather) 1–2

Undercliff 22, 23, 27, 38, 41, 65
Uplyme 27, *29,* 30, 32, 33, 51

Wanklyn, Cyril 36, 59–60
War, Second World 64–6
Ware Cliffs 22, 23, 63

Warren (now Mulberry), Rhode Lane 2
Whitchurch Canonicorum (church) 34, 42
White Gate 30
Willis family 11, 27
Wingrave, Dr Wyatt 60–61
Woodhouse Hill 27, 32, 33
Woodhouse Pinetum 37
Woodmead Halls 14
Woodroffe, Rex 39

Yawl 32